BANANAS!

A MY INCREDIBLE WORLD PICTURE BOOK

MY INCREDIBLE WORLD

Copyright © 2024, My Incredible World

All rights reserved. This book or any portion thereof may not be reproduced or used in any manner whatsoever without the express written permission of the copyright holder.

www.myincredibleworld.com

Bananas are one of the most popular fruits in the world, enjoyed by people everywhere.

Bananas grow on tall plants that look like trees, but they are actually large herbs!

Each plant produces a big bunch of bananas, some with more than 100!

Bananas grow in clusters called **hands**, with each banana being a **finger**.

They begin as bulbs, not seeds, and new plants sprout from the base of an old one!

Bananas start out green, and they turn yellow as they ripen and become sweeter.

They are rich in **potassium**, which is good for your muscles and heart.

The inside of a banana is soft and creamy, making it a great snack that's easy to eat.

They are grown in tropical regions, where it's warm and rainy, like in Central and South America.

There are over 1,000 types of bananas, but the most common one we eat is called the Cavendish.

They are picked while they're still green so they can ripen during their journey to stores.

11

Bananas are used to make many things like banana bread and smoothies.

In some countries, people eat them when they are green, cooking them as a savory dish.

Some people dry bananas to make banana chips, which are a crunchy and tasty snack.

In many places, people use banana leaves as plates or to wrap food for cooking.

Bananas are important to farmers in tropical countries, providing jobs and income.

They are also vital for people's health and for economies around the world.

Bananas can be a healthy part of breakfast, lunch, or a quick snack on the go.

The fiber in them helps keep your digestive system healthy and working well.

The word "banana" actually comes from an Arabic word that means "finger," because of its shape.

The peel protects the fruit inside and can also be used in compost to help other plants grow!

Bananas are incredible!

Made in the USA
Columbia, SC
10 February 2025